T0320574

AI FOR GAMES

AI FOR EVERYTHING

Artificial intelligence (AI) is all around us. From driverless cars to game-winning computers to fraud protection, AI is already involved in many aspects of life, and its impact will only continue to grow in the future. Many of the world's most valuable companies are investing heavily in AI research and development, and not a day goes by without news of cutting-edge breakthroughs in AI and robotics.

The *AI for Everything* series will explore the role of AI in contemporary life, from cars and aircraft to medicine, education, fashion, and beyond. Concise and accessible, each book is written by an expert in the field and will bring the study and reality of AI to a broad readership including interested professionals, students, researchers, and lay readers.

AI for Immunology
Louis J. Catania

AI for Cars
Hanky Sjafrie & Josep Aulinas

AI for Digital Warfare
Niklas Hageback & Daniel Hedblom

AI for Art
Niklas Hageback & Daniel Hedblom

AI for Creativity
Niklas Hageback

AI for Death and Dying
Maggi Savin-Baden

AI for Radiology
Oge Marques

AI for Games
Ian Millington

AI for School Teachers
Rose Luckin & Karine George

AI for Learners
Carmel Kent, Benedict du Boulay & Rose Luckin

AI for Social Justice
Alan Dix and Clara Crivellaro

For more information about this series please visit:
https://www.routledge.com/AI-for-Everything/book-series/AIFE

AI FOR GAMES

IAN MILLINGTON

CRC Press
Taylor & Francis Group
Boca Raton London New York

CRC Press is an imprint of the
Taylor & Francis Group, an **informa** business

First Edition published 2022
by CRC Press
6000 Broken Sound Parkway NW, Suite 300, Boca Raton, FL 33487-2742

and by CRC Press
2 Park Square, Milton Park, Abingdon, Oxon, OX14 4RN

© 2022 Ian Millington

CRC Press is an imprint of Taylor & Francis Group, LLC

Library of Congress Cataloging-in-Publication Data
Names: Millington, Ian, author.
Title: AI for games / Ian Millington.
Description: Fourth edition. | Boca Raton : CRC Press, 2022. |
Includes bibliographical references and index.
Identifiers: LCCN 2021027654 | ISBN 9780367643447 (hardback) |
ISBN 9780367643430 (paperback) | ISBN 9781003124047 (ebook)
Subjects: LCSH: Computer games—Programming. | Artificial intelligence. |
Computer animation.
Classification: LCC QA76.76.C672 M549 2022 | DDC 794.8/1525—dc23
LC record available at https://lccn.loc.gov/2021027654

ISBN: 978-0-367-64344-7 (hbk)
ISBN: 978-0-367-64343-0 (pbk)
ISBN: 978-1-003-12404-7 (ebk)

DOI: 10.1201/9781003124047

Typeset in Joanna
by codeMantra

CONTENTS

AUTHOR

Ian Millington is a British developer and author of books and courses on software development, particularly in the fields of artificial intelligence, decision support, and game physics engine development. Also an AJAX technology pioneer, Millington is attributed with creating a model of distributed power for management of a creative game with a troupe system style of play.

INTRODUCTION

Game development lives in its own technical world. It has its own idioms, skills, and challenges. That's one of the reasons games are so much fun to work on. Each game has its own rules, its own aesthetic, and its own trade-offs, and the hardware it will run on keeps changing. There's a reasonably good chance you will be the first person to meet and beat a new programming challenge.

Despite numerous efforts to standardize game development in line with the rest of the software industry (efforts that go back at least 25 years), the style of programming in a game is still rather unique. There is a focus on speed, but it differs from real-time programming for embedded or control applications. There is a focus on clever algorithms, but it doesn't share the same rigor as database server engineering. It draws techniques from a huge range of different sources, but almost without exception modifies them beyond resemblance. And, to add an extra layer of intrigue, developers make their modifications in different ways, often under extreme time pressure, and tailored entirely to the game at hand, leaving algorithms unrecognizable from studio to studio or project to project.

As exciting and challenging as this may be, it makes it difficult for new developers to get the information they need. Twenty years ago, it was almost impossible to get hold of information about techniques and algorithms that real developers used in their games. There was an atmosphere of secrecy, even alchemy, about the coding techniques in top studios. Then came the Internet and an ever-growing range of websites, along with books, conferences, and periodicals. It is now easier than ever to teach yourself new techniques in game development.

DOI: 10.1201/9781003124047-1

This book is designed to help you understand one element of game development: artificial intelligence (AI). There have been many articles published about different aspects of game AI and websites on particular techniques, compilations in book form, some introductory texts, and plenty of lectures at development conferences. A much more detailed discussion of the topics presented here can be found in my book *AI for Games, Third Edition* (CRC Press, 2019).

1

WHAT IS AI?

Artificial intelligence is about making computers able to perform the thinking tasks that humans and animals are capable of.

We can program computers to have superhuman abilities in solving many problems: arithmetic, sorting, searching, and so on. Some of these problems were originally considered AI problems, but as they have been solved in more and more comprehensive ways, they have slipped out of the domain of AI developers.

But there are many things that computers aren't good at which we find trivial: recognizing familiar faces, speaking our own language, deciding what to do next, and being creative. These are the domains of AI: trying to work out what kinds of algorithms are needed to display these properties.

Often the dividing line between AI and not-AI is merely difficulty: things we can't do require AI, things we can are tricks and math. It is tempting to get into a discussion of what is "real" AI, to try defining "intelligence," "consciousness," or "thought." In my experience, it is an impossible task, largely irrelevant to the business of making games.

In academia, some AI researchers are motivated by those philosophical questions: understanding the nature of thought and the nature of intelligence and building software to model how thinking might work. Others are motivated by psychology: understanding the mechanics of the human brain and mental processes. And yet

DOI: 10.1201/9781003124047-2

others are motivated by engineering: building algorithms to perform human-like tasks. This threefold distinction is at the heart of academic AI, and the different concerns are responsible for different subfields of the subject.

As games developers, we are practical folks, interested in only the engineering side. We build algorithms that make game characters appear human or animal-like. Developers have always drawn from academic research, where that research helps them get the job done, and ignored the rest.

It is worth taking a quick overview of the AI work done in academia to get a sense of what exists in the subject and what might be worth plagiarizing.

ACADEMIC AI

To tell the story, I will divide academic AI into three periods: the early days, the symbolic era, and the natural computing and statistical era. This is a gross oversimplification, of course, and they all overlap to some extent, but I find it a useful distinction.

THE EARLY DAYS

The early days include the time before computers, where philosophy of mind occasionally made forays into AI with such questions as: "What produces thought?" "Could you give life to an inanimate object?" "What is the difference between a cadaver and the human it previously was?" Tangential to this was the popular taste in automata, mechanical robots, from the 18th century onward. Intricate clockwork models were created that displayed the kind of animated, animal or human-like behaviors that we now employ game artists to create in a modeling package.

In the war effort of the 1940s, the need to break enemy codes and to perform the calculations required for atomic warfare motivated the development of the first programmable computers. Given that these machines were being used to perform calculations that would otherwise be done by a person, it was natural for programmers to be interested in AI. Several computing pioneers (such as Turing, von Neumann, and Shannon) were also pioneers in early AI.

THE SYMBOLIC ERA

From the late 1950s through to the early 1980s, the main thrust of AI research was "symbolic" systems. A symbolic system is one in which the algorithm is divided into two components: a set of knowledge (represented as symbols such as words, numbers, sentences, or pictures) and a reasoning algorithm that manipulates those symbols to create new combinations that hopefully represent problem solutions or new knowledge.

An expert system, one of the purest expressions of this approach, is among the most famous AI techniques. If today all the AI headlines talk about "deep learning," in the 1980s, they name dropped "expert systems." An expert system has a large database of knowledge, and it applies a collection of rules to draw conclusions or to discover new things. Other symbolic approaches applicable to games include blackboard architectures, pathfinding, decision trees, and state machines.

A common feature of symbolic systems is a trade-off: When solving a problem the more knowledge you have, the less work you need to do in reasoning. Often, reasoning algorithms consist of searching: trying different possibilities to get the best result. This leads us to the golden rule of AI:

> Search and knowledge are intrinsically linked. The more knowledge you have, the less searching for an answer you need; the more search you can do (i.e., the faster you can search), the less knowledge you need.

Some have suggested that knowledge-infused search (known as "heuristic search") is the way all intelligent behavior arises. Unfortunately, despite having several solid and important features, this theory has largely been discredited as an account of all intelligence. Nevertheless, many people with a recent education in AI are not aware that, as an engineering trade-off, knowledge versus search is unavoidable. At a practical level, AI engineers have always known it.

THE NATURAL COMPUTING/STATISTICAL ERA

Through the 1980s and into the early 1990s, there was an increasing frustration with symbolic approaches. The frustration came from various directions.

From an engineering point of view, the early successes on simple problems didn't seem to scale to more difficult problems. For example, it seemed easy to develop AI that understood (or appeared to understand) simple sentences, but developing an understanding of a full human language seemed no nearer. This was compounded by hype: When AI touted as "the next big thing" failed to live up to its billing, confidence in the whole sector crashed.

There was also an influential philosophical argument that symbolic approaches weren't biologically plausible. You can't understand how a human being plans a route by using a symbolic route-planning algorithm any more than you can understand how human muscles work by studying a forklift truck.

The effect was a move toward natural computing: techniques inspired by biology or other natural systems. These techniques include neural networks, genetic algorithms, and simulated annealing. Many natural computing techniques have been around for a long time.

But in the 1980s through to the early 2000s, they received the bulk of the research effort. When I began my PhD in artificial intelligence in the 1990s, it was difficult to find research places in Expert Systems, for example. I studied genetic algorithms; most of my peers were working on neural networks.

Despite its origin as a correlate to biology, AI research heavily applied mathematics, particularly probability and statistics, to understanding and optimizing natural computing techniques. The ability to handle all the uncertainty and messiness of real-world data, in contrast to the clean and rigid boundaries of the symbolic approaches, led to the development of a wide range of other probabilistic techniques, such as Bayes nets, support-vector machines (SVMs), and Gaussian processes.

The biggest change in AI in the last decade has not come from a breakthrough in academia. We are living in a time when AI is again back in the newspapers: self-driving cars, deep fakes, world champion Go programs, and home virtual assistants. This is the era of deep learning. Though many academic innovations are used, these systems are still fundamentally powered by neural networks, now made practical by the increase in computing power.

ENGINEERING

Though newspaper headlines and high-profile applications have flourished in the last 5 years, AI has been a key technology relevant to solving real-world problems for decades. Navigation systems in cars, job scheduling in factories, voice recognition and dictation, and large-scale search are all more than 20 years old. Google's search technology, for example, has long been underpinned by AI.

When something is hot, it is tempting to assume it is the only thing that matters. When natural computing techniques took center stage, there was a tendency to assume that symbolic approaches were dead. Similarly, with talk of deep learning everywhere, you might be forgiven for thinking that is what should be used.

But we always come back to the same trade-off: search vs knowledge. Deep learning is the ultimate in the compute-intensive search; AlphaGo Zero (the third iteration of the AlphaGo software) was given very minimal knowledge of the rules of the game, but extraordinary amounts of processing time to try different strategies and learn the best. On the other hand, a character that needs to use a health pack when injured can be told that explicitly:

```
IF injured THEN use health pack
```
No search required.

The only way any algorithm can outperform another is either to consume more processing power (more search), or to be optimized toward a specific set of problems (more knowledge of the problem).

In practice, engineers work from both sides. A voice recognition program, for example, converts the input signals using known formulae into a format where the neural network can decode it. The results are then fed through a series of symbolic algorithms that look at words from a dictionary and the way words are combined in the language. A statistical algorithm optimizing the order of a production line will have the rules about production encoded into its structure, so it can't possibly suggest an illegal timetable: The knowledge is used to reduce the amount of search required.

Unfortunately, games are usually designed to run on consumer hardware. And while AI is important, graphics have always taken the majority of the processing power. This seems in no danger of changing. For AI designed to run on the device during the game, low computation/high knowledge approaches are often the clear winners. And these are very often symbolic: approaches pioneered in academia in the 1970s and 1980s.

GAME AI

Pac-Man was the first game many people remember playing with fledgling AI. Up to that point, there had been Pong clones with opponent-controlled bats (following the ball up and down) and countless shooters in the Space Invaders mold. But Pac-Man had definite enemy characters that seemed to conspire against you, moved around the level just as you did, and made life tough.

Pac-Man relied on a very simple AI technique: a state machine. Each of the four monsters (later called ghosts after a disastrously flickering port to the Atari 2600) occupied one of three states: chasing, scattering (heading for the corners at specific time intervals), and frightened (when Pac-Man eats a power-up). For each state, they choose a tile as their target and turn toward it at each junction. In chase mode, each ghost chooses the target according to a slightly different hard-coded rule, giving them their personalities.

Game AI didn't change much until the mid-1990s. Most computer-controlled characters prior to then were about as sophisticated as a Pac-Man ghost.

Take a classic like Golden Axe eight years later. Enemy characters stood still (or walked back and forward a short distance) until the player got close to them, whereupon they homed in on the player. Golden Axe had a neat innovation with enemies that would enter a running state to rush past the player and then switch back to homing mode, attacking from behind. Surrounding the player looks impressive, but the underlying AI is no more complex than Pac-Man.

In the mid-1990s, AI began to be a selling point for games. Games like Beneath a Steel Sky even mentioned AI on the back of the box. Unfortunately, its much-hyped "Virtual Theater" AI system simply allowed characters to walk backward and forward through the game—hardly a real advancement.

Goldeneye 007 probably did the most to show gamers what AI could do to improve gameplay. Still relying on characters with a small number of well-defined states, Goldeneye added a sense simulation system: Characters could see their colleagues and would notice if they were killed. Sense simulation was the topic of the moment, with Thief: The Dark Project and Metal Gear Solid basing their whole game design on the technique.

In the mid-1990s, real-time strategy (RTS) games also were beginning to take off. World of WarCraft was one of the first times pathfinding was widely noticed in action (though it had been used several times before). AI researchers were working with emotional models of soldiers in a military battlefield simulation in 1998 when they saw Warhammer: Dark Omen doing the same thing. It was also one of the first times people saw robust formation motion in action.

Halo introduced decision trees, now a standard method for characters to decide what to do. F.E.A.R. used goal-oriented action planning (GOAP) for the same purpose. With the success of AlphaGo, deep learning has become a hot topic, though it is still only practicable offline.

Some games are designed around the AI. *Creatures* did this in 1997, but games like *The Sims* and its sequels, or *Black & White* have carried on the torch. Creatures still has one of the most complex AI systems seen in a game, with a simulated hormone system and a neural network-based brain for each creature.

Games like *Half-Life* and *The Last of Us* use AI-controlled characters to collaborate with the player, meaning they are on screen for much longer, and any faults are much more noticeable.

First-person shooters and RTS games have been subjected to significant academic research (there is an annual competition for *StarCraft* AI, for example). RTS games incorporate AI techniques used in military simulation (to the extent that *Full Spectrum Warrior* started life as a military training simulator).

Sports games and driving games in particular have their own AI challenges, some of which remain largely unsolved (dynamically calculating the fastest way around a race track, for example, would also be helpful to motorsport teams), while role-playing games (RPGs) with complex character interactions still implemented as conversation trees feel overdue for something better (interesting and sophisticated conversation AI has been implemented in games such as *Façade* and *Blood and Laurels*, the one released game using the short-lived Versu game engine).

We have come a long way, certainly. But, though we have a massive diversity of AI in games, many genres are still using the simple AI of 1979 because that's all they need.

The AI in most games addresses three basic needs: the ability to move characters, the ability to make decisions about where to move, and the ability to think tactically or strategically. Even though we have a broad range of approaches, they all fulfill the same three basic requirements.

2

MODEL OF GAME AI

There is a vast zoo of algorithms and techniques in game AI. It would be easy to get lost, so it's important to understand how the bits fit together. To help, I've used a consistent structure to contextualize the AI used in a game. This isn't the only possible model, and it isn't the only model that would benefit from the techniques in this book.

Figure 2.1 illustrates this model. It splits the AI task into three sections: movement, decision-making, and strategy. The first two sections contain algorithms that work on a character-by-character basis, and the last section operates on a team or side. Around these three AI elements is a whole set of additional infrastructure.

Not all game applications require all levels of AI. Board games like Chess or Risk require only the strategy level; the characters in the game (if they can even be called that) don't make their own decisions and don't need to worry about how to move.

On the other hand, there is no strategy at all in many games. Non-player characters in a platform game, such as *Hollow Knight* or *Super Mario Bros.*, are purely reactive, making their own simple decisions and acting on them. There is no coordination that makes sure the enemy characters do the best job of thwarting the player.

DOI: 10.1201/9781003124047-3

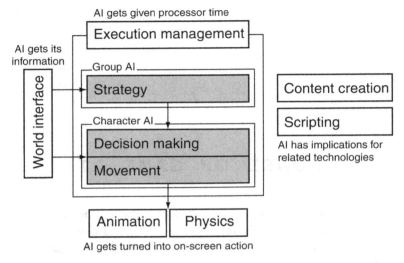

Figure 2.1 The AI model.

MOVEMENT

Movement refers to algorithms that turn decisions into some kind of motion. When an enemy character without a projectile attack needs to attack the player in *Super Mario Sunshine*, it first heads directly for the player. When it is close enough, it can actually do the attacking. The decision to attack is carried out by a set of movement algorithms that home in on the player's location. Only then can the attack animation be played and the player's health be depleted.

Movement algorithms can be more complex than simply homing in. A character may need to avoid obstacles on the way or even work their way through a series of rooms. A guard in some levels of *Splinter Cell* will respond to the appearance of the player by raising an alarm. This may require navigating to the nearest wall-mounted alarm point, which can be a long distance away and may involve complex navigation around obstacles or through corridors.

Lots of actions are carried out using animation directly. If a Sim, in *The Sims*, is sitting by the table with food in front of her and wants to carry out an eating action, then the eating animation is simply played. Once the AI has decided that the character should eat, no more AI is needed (the animation technology used is not covered in this book). If the same character is by the back door when she wants to eat, however, movement AI needs to guide her to the chair (or to some other nearby source of food).

DECISION-MAKING

Decision-making involves a character working out what to do next. Typically, each character has a range of different behaviors that they could choose to perform: attacking, standing still, hiding, exploring, patrolling, and so on. The decision-making system needs to work out which of these behaviors is the most appropriate at each moment of the game. The chosen behavior can then be executed using movement AI and animation technology.

At its simplest, a character may have very simple rules for selecting a behavior. The farm animals in various levels of the *Legend of Zelda* games will stand still unless the player gets too close, whereupon they will move away a small distance.

At the other extreme, enemies in *Half-Life* 2 display complex decision-making, where they will try a number of different strategies to reach the player: chaining together intermediate actions such as throwing grenades and laying down suppression fire in order to achieve their goals.

Some decisions may require movement AI to carry them out. A melee (hand-to-hand) attack will require the character to get close to its victim. In combat-heavy games such as *Dark Souls*, decision-making moves the character toward their target and also determines which attack, and thus which animation, is performed. In other games, once the decision is made, a predetermined animation is played without any additional movement (a Sim eating, for example) or the state of the game is directly modified without any kind of visual feedback (when a country AI in *Sid Meier's Civilization VI* elects to research a new technology, for example, it simply happens with no visual feedback to the player).

STRATEGY

You can go a long way with movement AI and decision-making AI, and most action-based three-dimensional (3D) games use only these two elements. But to coordinate a whole team, some strategic AI is required.

In the context of this book, strategy refers to an overall approach used by a group of characters. In this category are AI algorithms that don't control just one character, but influence the behavior of a whole set of characters. Each character in the group may (and usually will) have their own decision-making and movement algorithms, but overall, their decision-making will be influenced by a group strategy.

In the original *Half-Life*, enemies worked as a team to surround and eliminate the player. One would often rush past the player to take up a flanking position. This has been followed in more recent games, such as the evolving AI engine in the *Medal of Honor* franchise. Over time, we have seen increasing sophistication in the kinds of strategic actions that a team of enemies can carry out.

INFRASTRUCTURE

AI algorithms on their own are only half of the story, however. In order to actually build AI for a game, we'll need a whole set of additional infrastructure. The movement requests need to be turned into action in the game by using either animation or, increasingly, physics simulation.

Similarly, the AI needs information from the game to make sensible decisions. This is sometimes called "perception" (especially in academic AI): working out what information the character knows. In practice, it is much broader than just simulating what each character can see or hear, but includes all interfaces between the game world and the AI. This world interfacing is often a significant proportion of the work done by an AI programmer, and in my experience, it is a large proportion of the AI debugging effort.

Finally, the whole AI system needs to be managed so that it uses the right amount of processor time and memory. While some kind of execution management typically exists for each area of the game (level of detail algorithms for rendering, for example), managing the AI raises a whole set of techniques and algorithms of its own.

Each of these components may be thought of as being out of the remit of the AI developer. Sometimes they are (in particular, the animation system is often part of the graphics engine, or increasingly has its own dedicated programmers), but they are so crucial to getting the AI working that they can't be avoided altogether.

AGENT-BASED AI

I don't use the term "agents" very much in this book, even though the model I've described is an agent-based model.

In this context, agent-based AI is about producing autonomous characters that take in information from the game data, determine what actions to take based on the information, and carry out those actions.

It can be seen as bottom-up design: You start by working out how each character will behave and by implementing the AI needed to support that. The overall behavior of the game is then a function of how the individual character behaviors work together. The first two elements of the AI model we'll use, movement and decision-making, make up the AI for an agent in the game.

In contrast, a non-agent-based AI seeks to work out how everything ought to act from the top down and builds a single system to simulate everything. An example is the traffic and pedestrian simulation in the cities of *Grand Theft Auto 3*. The overall traffic and pedestrian flows are calculated based on the time of day and city region and are only turned into individual cars and people when the player can see them.

The distinction is hazy, however. A good AI developer will mix and match any reliable techniques that get the job done, regardless of the approach. That pragmatic approach is the one I always follow. So, I avoid using agent-based terminology and prefer to talk about game characters in general, however they are structured.

3

ALGORITHMS AND DATA STRUCTURES

There are three key elements to implementing game AI techniques: the algorithm itself, the data structures that the algorithm depends on, and the way the game world is represented to the algorithm (often encoded as an appropriate data structure).

ALGORITHMS

Algorithms are step-by-step processes that generate a solution to an AI problem. For example algorithms that generate routes through a game level to reach a goal, algorithms that work out which direction to move to intercept a fleeing enemy, and algorithms that learn what the player should do next.

Data structures are the other side of the coin to algorithms. They hold data in such a way that an algorithm can rapidly manipulate it to reach a solution. Often, data structures need to be tuned for one particular algorithm, and their execution speeds are intrinsically linked.

You will need to know a set of elements to implement and tune an algorithm, and these include:

DOI: 10.1201/9781003124047-4

- The problem that the algorithm tries to solve
- A general description of how the solution works, including diagrams where they are needed
- A pseudo-code presentation of the algorithm
- An indication of the data structures required to support the algorithm, including pseudo-code, where required
- Implementation advice, where needed
- Analysis of the algorithm performance: its execution speed, memory footprint, and scalability
- Weaknesses in the approach

PERFORMANCE CHARACTERISTICS

Execution speed and memory consumption often depend on the size of the problem being considered. The standard $O()$ notation is used to indicate the order of the most significant element in this scaling.

An algorithm might be described as being $O(n \log n)$ in execution and $O(n)$ in memory, where n is usually some kind of component of the problem, such as the number of other characters in the area, or the number of power-ups in the level.

A good text on general algorithms for computer science will give a full mathematical treatment of how $O()$ values are arrived at and the implications they have for the real-world performance of an algorithm.

Some algorithms have misleading performance characteristics. It is possible to set up highly improbable situations to deliberately make them perform poorly. In regular use (and certainly in any use you're likely to have in a game), they will have much better performance.

PSEUDO-CODE

Algorithms are often presented in pseudo-code for brevity and simplicity. Pseudo-code is an imaginary programming language that cuts out any implementation details particular to any real programming language. It should describe the algorithm in sufficient detail so you can implement it in the language of your choice.

Many AI algorithms need to work with relatively sophisticated data structures: lists, tables, priority queues, associative arrays, and so on. Some languages provide these built-in; others make them available as libraries, or accessed through functions. To make what is going on clearer, the pseudo-code treats these data structures as if they were part of the language, simplifying the code significantly.

As an example, the following sample is pseudo-code for a simple algorithm to select the highest value from an unsorted array:

```
function maximum(array:float[]) -> float:
    max: float = array[0]
    for element in array[1..]:
        if element > max:
            max = element
    return max
```

REPRESENTATIONS

Information in the game often needs to be turned into a suitable format for use by the AI. Often, this means converting it to a different representation or data structure. The game might store the level as meshes of 3D geometry and the character positions as (x, y, z) locations in the world.

Converting between these representations is a critical process because it often loses information (that's the point: to simplify out the irrelevant details), and you always run the risk of losing the wrong bits of data. Choosing the correct representation is a key element of implementing AI, and certain representations are particularly important in game AI.

Although very similar to a data structure, we will often not worry directly about how the representation is implemented, but instead will focus on the interface it presents to the AI code. This makes it easier for you to integrate the AI techniques into your game, simply by creating the right glue code to turn your game data into the representation needed by the algorithms.

For example, imagine we want to work out if a character feels healthy or not as part of some algorithm for determining its actions. We might simply require a representation of the character with a method we can call:

```
class Character:
    # Return true if the character feels healthy,
and false otherwise.
    function feelsHealthy() -> bool
```

You may then implement this by checking against the character's health score, by keeping a Boolean "healthy" value for each character, or even by running a whole algorithm to determine the character's psychological state and its perception of its own health. As far as the decision making routine is concerned, it doesn't matter how the value is being generated.

The pseudo-code defines an interface (in the object-oriented sense) that can be implemented in any way you choose.

IMPLEMENTATION

Even a decade ago, most developers used C++ for their AI code. A decade before that, a significant number relied on C. Games development is much more varied now: Swift and Java for mobile platforms, C# for the unity game engine, and JavaScript on the web. There are many other languages used here and there in game development: Lisp, Lua, or Python, particularly as scripting languages; ActionScript for the few remaining Flash developers. I've personally worked with all these languages at one point or another, so I've tried to be as language independent as possible, while still giving some advice on implementation.

Of these, C and C++ are still used for code that absolutely, positively has to run as fast as possible. In places, some of the discussion of data structures and optimizations will focus on C++, because the optimizations are C++ specific.

4

GAME AI

This chapter looks at the high-level issues around game AI: What kinds of approaches work, what they need to take account of, and how they can all be put together.

THE COMPLEXITY FALLACY

It is a common mistake to think that the more complex the AI in a game, the better the characters will look to the player. Creating good AI is all about matching the requirements of the game to the right behaviors and the right algorithms to produce them. There is a bewildering array of techniques, and the right one isn't always the most obvious choice.

Countless examples of difficult-to-implement, complex AI have resulted in poor, or even stupid-looking behavior. Equally, a very simple technique can be perfect, when used well.

WHEN SIMPLE THINGS LOOK GOOD

As mentioned earlier, Pac-Man was one of the first games with any form of character AI. The AI has three states: one normal state when the player is collecting pips; a second state when the player has eaten the power-up and is out for revenge; and a final state that triggers at timed intervals, to have the ghosts back off a little.

DOI: 10.1201/9781003124047-5

In all three states, each of the four ghosts has a target. It moves in a straight line until it reaches a junction, then chooses whichever route is closest to the direction of its target. It doesn't attempt to plan the entire route, or even check its target can be reached, it just moves toward it. In their chasing state, when hunting the player, each ghost has its own simple snippet of code to choose a target. Blinky (the red ghost) always targets the player position. Pinky (the pink one, obviously) targets a square four spaces in front of the player, even if that is inside or on the other side of a wall. Inky (light blue) uses a modified offset of its own and the player's position. Clyde (orange) targets the player if they are far away, or the corner of the board if close. All these targeting routines can be implemented in a line or two of code.

This is about as simple as you can imagine an AI for a moving character. Any simpler and the ghosts would be either very predictable (if they always homed in) or purely random. On their own, the ghosts strategy can be easily predicted; their AI does not pose a challenge. But together, the different behaviors of each ghost are enough to make a significant opposing force—so much so that the AI to this day gets flattering comments. For example, this comment recently appeared on a website: "To give the game some tension, some clever AI was programmed into the game. The ghosts would group up, attack the player, then disperse. Each ghost had its own AI."

Other players have reported strategies among the ghosts: "The four of them are programmed to set a trap, with Blinky leading the player into an ambush where the other three lie in wait."

A simple AI, done well, can appear to a player to be much more intelligent than it is.

The same thing has been reported by many other developers on own their games. As an extreme example, a few years ago Chris Kingsley of Rebellion mentioned an unpublished Nintendo Game Boy title in which particular enemy characters simply home in on the player, but for variation, sidestep at random intervals as they move forward. Players reported that these characters "anticipated" their firing patterns and dodged out of the way.

The AI wasn't anticipating anything, and only managed to dodge by coincidence some of the time. But a timely sidestep at a crucial moment stayed in the player's mind and shaped their perception of the AI.

WHEN COMPLEX THINGS LOOK BAD

Of course, the opposite thing can easily happen. A game that I looked forward to immensely was *Herdy Gerdy*, one of the launch games Sony used to tout the new gameplay possibilities of the "emotion engine" chip in their PlayStation 2 hardware. The game is a herding game. An ecosystem of characters is present in the game level. The player has to herd individuals of different species into their corresponding pens. Herding had been used before and has since as a component of a bigger game, but in *Herdy Gerdy*, it constituted all of the gameplay.

Unfortunately, the characters' movement AI was not quite up to the challenge of its rich level design. It was easy to get them caught on the scenery, and their collision detection could leave them stuck in irretrievable places. This would be frustrating (though not uncommon) in any game. But it interacted with the herding AI in a way that made some characters appear unexpectedly unintelligent. Reviews were mixed, and sales lackluster.

Unlike *Herdy Gerdy*, *Black & White* achieved significant sales success. But at places it also suffered from great AI looking bad. The game involves teaching a character what to do by a combination of example and feedback. When people first play through the game, they often end up inadvertently teaching the creature bad habits, and in the worst cases, it may become unable to carry out even the most basic actions. By paying more attention to how the creature's AI works, players are able to manipulate it better, but the illusion of teaching a real creature can be gone.

Most of the complex things I've seen that looked bad never made it to the final game. It is a perennial temptation for developers to use the latest techniques and the most hyped algorithms to implement their character AI. Late in development, when a learning AI still can't learn how to steer a car around a track without driving off at every corner, simpler algorithms come to the rescue and make it into the game's release.

Knowing when to be complex and when to stay simple is the most difficult element of the game AI programmer's art. The best AI programmers are those who can use a very simple technique to give the illusion of complexity.

This is easier when there is a tight feedback loop between implementation and game design. A slight modification to the requirements can mean a better AI technique can be used, which leads to a better game. Sometimes this means making the required behavior simpler, to make it much more robust. Unfortunately, with the large team sizes on mass-market PC and console games, it is difficult for a programmer to have much influence. Indie and mobile games, whose teams are much smaller, though not as small as they were a few years ago, still have more opportunity.

THE PERCEPTION WINDOW

Unless your AI is controlling an ever-present sidekick or a one-on-one enemy, chances are your player will only come across a character for a short time.

This can be a significantly short time for disposable guards whose life purpose is to be shot. More difficult enemies can be on-screen for a few minutes as their downfall is plotted and executed.

When we seek to understand someone in real life, we naturally put ourselves into their shoes. We look at their surroundings, the information they are gleaning from their environment, and the actions they are carrying out. The same happens with game characters. A guard standing in a dark room hears a noise: "I'd flick the light switch," we think. If the guard doesn't do that, we might assume they are stupid.

If we only catch a glimpse of someone for a short while, we don't have enough time to understand their situation. If we see a guard who has heard a noise suddenly turn away and move slowly in the opposite direction, we assume the AI is faulty. The guard should have moved across the room toward the noise. If we observed them for longer to see the guard head over to a light switch by the exit, their action would be understandable. Then again, the guard might not flick on the light switch after all, and we might take that as a sign of poor implementation. But the guard may know that the light is inoperable, or they may have been waiting for a colleague to slip some cigarettes under the door and thought the noise was a predefined signal. If we knew all that, we'd know the action was intelligent after all.

This no-win situation is the perception window. You need to make sure that a character's AI matches its purpose in the game and the attention it will get from the player. Adding more AI to incidental characters might endear you to the rare gamer who spends hours analyzing each level, checking for curious behavior or bugs, but everyone else (including the publisher and the press) may think your programming was sloppy.

CHANGES OF BEHAVIOR

The perception window isn't only about time. Think about the ghosts in *Pac-Man* again. They might not give the impression of sentience, but they don't do anything out of place. This is because they rarely change behavior (the most noticeable is their transformation when the player eats a power-up).

Whenever a character in a game changes behavior, the change is far more conspicuous than the behavior itself. In the same way, when a character's behavior should obviously change and doesn't, it draws attention. If two guards are standing talking to each other and you shoot one down, the other guard shouldn't carry on the conversation!

A change in behavior almost always occurs when the player is nearby or has been spotted. This is the same in platform games as it is in real-time strategy. A good solution is to keep only two behaviors for incidental characters—a normal action and a player-spotted action.

THE KIND OF AI IN GAMES

Games have always come under criticism for being poorly programmed, in a software engineering sense: They use tricks, arcane optimizations, and unproven technologies to get extra speed or neat effects. Though game engines may be reused, gameplay code usually isn't (or at least isn't written with that in mind) and strong time pressures mean programmers often do whatever they need to get the game done. Game AI is no different.

There is a big gulf between what qualifies as AI in games (i.e., what is the responsibility of an AI programmer) and what the rest of the programming industry or academia considers to be AI.

In my experience, AI for a game is equal parts hacking (*ad hoc* solutions and neat effects), heuristics (rules of thumb that only work in most, but not all, cases), and algorithms (the "proper" stuff). The last group are the techniques we can generalize, examine analytically, use in multiple games, and build into an AI engine.

But *ad hoc* solutions and heuristics are just as important and can breathe as much life into characters as the most complicated algorithm.

HACKS

There's a saying that goes "If it looks like a fish and swims like a fish, it's probably a fish." We understand a behavior by replicating it to a sufficient accuracy.

As a psychological approach, it has some pedigree (it is related to the behaviorist school of psychology), but has largely been superseded. This fall from fashion has influenced psychological approaches to AI, as well. At one point, it was quite acceptable to learn about human intelligence by making a machine to replicate it, but now that is considered poor science. And with good reason, after all, building a machine to play skillful Chess involves algorithms that evaluate millions of board positions. Human beings are simply not capable of this.

On the other hand, as AI engineers, we are not paid to be interested in the nature of reality or mind; we want characters that look right. In most cases, this means starting from human behaviors and trying to work out the easiest way to implement them in software.

Good AI in games usually works in this direction. Developers rarely build a great new algorithm and then ask themselves, "so what can I do with this?" Instead, you start with a design for a character and apply the most relevant tool to get the result.

This means that what qualifies as game AI may be unrecognizable as an AI technique. A simple random number generator applied judiciously can produce a lot of believability. Generating a random number isn't an AI technique as such. In most languages, there are built-in functions to get a random number, so there is certainly no point giving an algorithm for it! But it can work in a surprising number of situations.

Another good example of creative AI development is *The Sims*. While there are reasonably complicated things going on under the surface, a lot of the character behavior is communicated with animation. Remove the character animation, and the AI would look far less impressive. In *StarWars Episode 1: Racer*, characters who are annoyed gave a little sideswipe to other characters. *Quake II* introduced the "gesture" command, now used in a vast range of first-person games, where characters (and players) can flip their enemy off. All these require no significant AI infrastructure. They don't need complicated cognitive models, learning, or neural networks. They just need a few lines of code that schedule an animation at the appropriate time.

Always be on the lookout for simple things that can give the illusion of intelligence. If you want engaging emotional characters, is it possible to add a couple of emotion animations (a frustrated rub of the temple, perhaps, or a stamp of the foot) to your game? Triggering these in the right place is much easier than trying to represent the character's emotional state through their actions. Do you have a portfolio of behaviors that the character will choose from? Will the choice involve complex weighing of many factors? If so, it might be worth trying a version of the AI that picks a behavior purely at random (maybe with different probabilities for each behavior). You might be able to tell the difference, but your customers may not; so try it out before you code the complex version.

HEURISTICS

A heuristic is a rule of thumb, an approximate solution that might work in many situations but is unlikely to work in all.

Human beings use heuristics all the time. We don't try to work out all the consequences of our actions. Instead, we rely on general principles that we've found to work in the past (or that we have been taught or even brainwashed with, equally). It might range from something as simple as "if you lose something then retrace your steps to look for it" to heuristics that govern our life choices, such as "never trust a used-car salesman."

Heuristics have been codified and incorporated into some of the algorithms in this book, and saying "heuristic" to an AI programmer often conjures up images of pathfinding or goal-oriented behaviors. Beyond these, many of the techniques in this book rely on heuristics that may not always be explicit. There is a trade-off between speed and accuracy in areas such as decision-making, movement, and tactical thinking (including board game AI). When accuracy is sacrificed, it is usually by replacing search for a correct answer with a heuristic.

A wide range of heuristics can be applied to general AI problems that don't require a particular algorithm.

In our perennial *Pac-Man* example, the ghosts move by taking the route at a junction that leads toward their current target. They don't attempt to calculate the best route: either the shortest or fastest. That might be quite complex and involve turning back on oneself, and it might be ultimately redundant as the position of the player continues to change. But the rule of thumb (move in the current direction of the target) works most of the time and provides sufficient competence for the player to understand that the ghosts aren't purely random in their motion.

In *World of WarCraft* (and many other RTS games that followed), there is a heuristic that moves a character forward slightly so they can engage an enemy standing a fraction beyond the character's reach. While this worked in most cases, it wasn't always the best option. Many players got frustrated as comprehensive defensive structures went walkabout when enemies came close. Later, RTS games allowed the player to choose whether this behavior was switched on or not.

In many strategic games, including board games, different units or pieces are given a single numeric value to represent how "good" they are. In Chess, pawns are often given one point, bishops and knights three, rooks five, and the queen eight. This is a heuristic; it replaces complex calculations about the capabilities of a unit with a single number. And the number can be defined by the programmer in advance. The AI can work out which side is ahead simply by adding the numbers. In an RTS, it can find the best value offensive unit to build by comparing the number with the cost. A lot of useful effects can be achieved just by manipulating the number.

There isn't an algorithm or a technique for this. And you won't find it in published AI research. But it is the bread and butter of an AI programmer's job.

COMMON HEURISTICS

A handful of heuristics appear over and over. They are good starting points when initially tackling a problem.

MOST CONSTRAINED

Given the current state of the world, one item in a set needs to be chosen. The item chosen should be the one that would be an option for the fewest number of states.

For example, a squad of characters engages a group of enemies. One of the enemies is wearing a type of armor that only one rifle can penetrate. One squad member has this rifle. When they select who to attack, the most constrained heuristic comes into play; only one squad member can attack this enemy, so that is the action that they should take. Even if their weapon would be more powerful against different enemy, their squad mates should handle the others.

DO THE MOST DIFFICULT THING FIRST

The hardest thing to do often has implications for lots of other actions. It is better to do this first, rather than find that the easy stuff goes well but is ultimately wasted.

For example, an army has two squads with empty slots. The computer schedules the creation of five Orc warriors and a huge Stone Troll. It wants to end up with balanced squads. How should it assign the units to squads? The Stone Troll requires the most slots, so is the hardest to assign. It should be placed first.

If the Orcs were assigned first, they would be balanced between the two squads, leaving room for half a Troll in each squad, but nowhere for the Troll to go.

TRY THE MOST PROMISING THING FIRST

If there are a number of options open to the AI, it is often possible to give each one a really rough-and-ready score. Even if this score is dramatically inaccurate, trying the options in decreasing score order will provide better performance than trying things purely at random.

ALGORITHMS

And so we come to the final third of the AI programmer's job: building algorithms to support interesting character behavior. Hacks and heuristics will get you a long way, but relying on them solely means you'll have to constantly reinvent the wheel. General bits of AI, such as movement, decision-making, and tactical thinking, all benefit from tried and tested methods that can be endlessly reused.

Just remember that for every situation where a complex algorithm is the best way to go, there are likely to be several more where a simpler hack or heuristic will get the job done.

SPEED AND MEMORY CONSTRAINTS

The biggest constraint on the AI developer's job is the physical limitations of the machine. Game AI doesn't have the luxury of days of processing time and terabytes of memory. We don't even have the luxury of using all the processor and memory of the computer the game is running on. Other tasks need space and time, such as graphics, sound, networking, and input. In teams where different groups of developers have to work on their specialties in parallel, a speed and memory budget will be set.

One of the reasons AI techniques from academia or commercial research don't achieve widespread use is their processing time or memory requirements. An algorithm that might be compelling in a simple demo can slow a production game to a standstill.

This section looks at low-level hardware issues related to the design and construction of AI code. Most of what is contained here is general advice for all game code.

PROCESSOR ISSUES

The most obvious limitation on the efficiency of a game is the speed of the processor on which it is running. Originally, all the games machines had a single main processor, which was also responsible for graphics. Most game hardware now has several CPUs (several processing cores on the same piece of silicon, usually), and dedicated GPUs for processing graphics.

As a general rule, CPUs are faster and more flexible, where a GPU is more parallel. When the task can be split up into many simple subtasks, all running at the same time, the tens up to thousands of processing cores on a GPU can be orders of magnitude faster than the same task running sequentially on the CPU.

Graphics card drivers used to have "fixed function" pipelines, where the graphics code was built into the driver, and could only be tweaked within narrow parameters. It was impossible to do very much other than graphics on the graphics card. Now drivers support technologies such as Vulkan, DirectX 11, CUDA, and OpenCL, which allow general-purpose code to be executed on the GPU. As a result, more functionality has been moved to the GPU, freeing up more processing power on the CPU.

The share of the processing time dedicated to AI has grown in fits and starts over the last two decades, in some cases now making up most of the CPU load, with some AI running on the GPU. Along with the increase in processor speeds, this is obviously good news for AI developers wanting to apply more complicated algorithms, particularly to decision-making and strategizing. But, while incremental improvements in processor time help unlock new techniques, they don't solve the underlying problem. Many AI algorithms take a long time to run. A comprehensive pathfinding system can take tens of milliseconds to run per character. Clearly, in an RTS with 1000 characters, there is no chance of running each frame. Complex AI that does work in games needs to be split into bite-size components that can be distributed over multiple frames. The chapter on resource management shows how to accomplish this. Applying these techniques to many long-running AI algorithms can bring them into the realm of practicality.

LOW-LEVEL CONCERNS

One large change in the industry in the last 10 years has been the move away from C++ having a hegemony over game programming. Now, character behavior, game logic, and AI are often written in higher-level languages such as C#, Swift, Java, or even scripting languages. This is significant because these languages provide the programmer less ability to micromanage the performance characteristics of their code. There are AI programmers still working in C++, who still need a good knowledge of the "bare metal" performance characteristics of the processors, but in my recent experience, such programmers tend to be low-level specialists working on AI engines: portfolios of functionality designed to be reused in multiple games.

I will describe three low-level issues briefly: SIMD, superscalar architectures, and virtual functions. In this edition, I will describe them only briefly. In my own professional practice, I haven't been directly concerned with any of these for several years.

SIMD (single instruction, multiple data) are a set of registers on modern hardware large enough to fit several floating point numbers. Mathematical operators can be applied to these registers, which has the effect of running the same code against multiple pieces of data in parallel. This can dramatically speed up some code, particularly geometric reasoning. Although CPUs have dedicated registers for SIMD, they provide the best speedup on code that tends to suit the GPU. Optimizing for SIMD on the CPU is often redundant, when the code can be moved onto the GPU.

Superscalar CPUs have several execution paths active at the same time. Code is split among the parts to execute in parallel, and the results are then recombined into the final result. When the result of one pipeline depends on another, this can involve either waiting, or guessing what the result might be and redoing the work if it proves to be wrong (known as *branch prediction*). In the last decade, multi-core CPUs, where several independent CPUs allow different threads to run in parallel, have become almost ubiquitous. Although each core may still be superscalar, this is now largely treated as a behind-the-scenes detail, irrelevant to AI programmers. Better speedups can be attained by concentrating on making AI code parallelizable, rather than worrying about the details of branch prediction.

AI code can take advantage of this parallelism either by running AI for different characters in different threads or by running all AI in a different thread to other game systems. These threads will then be executed in parallel on different cores, when available. Multiple threads doing the same thing (such as one character running its AI in each thread) are often more performant, as it is easier to make sure all processors are being used to the same capacity, and more flexible, as it scales without rebalancing to hardware with a different number of cores.

When AI routinely had to be careful of every single CPU cycle used, it was common to avoid virtual classes in C++, with their virtual function call overhead. This meant avoiding object-oriented polymorphism, whenever possible. A virtual function call stores the memory location in which the function is implemented in a variable (in a structure called a function table, or vtable). Calling a function therefore involves looking up the variable at runtime, and then looking up the location that variable specifies. Though this extra lookup uses a trivial amount of time, it could interact significantly with the branch predictor and processor cache. For this reason, virtual functions, and hence polymorphism, had a bad reputation. A reputation that has largely faded in the past 10 years. Now, game engines such as Unity, Unreal, Lumberyard, and Godot assume that game logic will be polymorphic.

MEMORY CONCERNS

Most AI algorithms do not require a large amount of RAM, often just a few, up to tens of megabytes. This small storage requirement, easily achievable on modest mobile devices, is ample for heavyweight algorithms such as terrain analysis and pathfinding. Massively multi-player online games (MMOGs) typically require much more storage for their larger worlds, but are run on server farms where sufficient memory can be installed (even then, we are only talking gigabytes of RAM, rarely more). Huge worlds are usually sharded into separate sections, or else characters are limited to certain areas, further reducing the AI memory requirements.

So it is not the amount of memory which is usually the limiting factor, but the way it is used. Allocation and cache coherence are both memory concerns that affect performance. They can both influence the implementation of an AI algorithm.

ALLOCATION AND GARBAGE COLLECTION

Allocation is the process of asking for memory in which to place data. When that memory is no longer needed, it is said to be freed or deallocated. Allocation and deallocation are relatively fast, as long as memory is available.

Low-level languages such as C require the programmer to free memory manually. Languages such as C++ and Swift, when memory is allocated for a particular object, provide "reference counting." This stores the number of places that know about the existence of the object. When the object is no longer referenced, the counter drops to 0, and the memory is freed. Unfortunately, both these approaches can mean that memory that should be freed is never freed. Either the programmer forgets to free manually, or there is a circular set of references, such that their counters never drop to 0. Many higher-level languages implement sophisticated algorithms to collect this "garbage," i.e., free memory that is no longer useful. Unfortunately, garbage collection can be expensive. In languages such as C#, particularly in the Mono runtime that runs the Unity game engine, garbage collection can be slow enough to delay a rendering frame, causing a visual stutter. This is unacceptable to most developers.

As a result, implementing AI algorithms for higher-level languages often involves trying not to allocate and deallocate objects while a level is running. The data required for the entire level are reserved when the level begins, and only released when the level ends. Several of the algorithms in this book assume that new objects can be created at any time, and will be left to disappear when no longer needed. On a platform with time-consuming garbage collection, it may be important to modify these implementations. When the path is complete, none of the intermediate location data are needed. A garbage-collection-friendly implementation might create a single pathfinding object, containing data for every location in the map. That same object is called whenever pathfinding is required, and it uses the preallocated location data it needs and ignores the rest. On its own, this implementation will be a little more complicated and could be considerably more complex if multiple characters who need pathfinding must queue to use the one pathfinding object.

CACHE

Memory size alone isn't the only limitation on memory use. The time it takes to access memory from the RAM and prepare it for use by the processor is significantly longer than the time it takes for the processor to perform its operations. If processors had to rely on the main RAM, they'd be constantly stalled waiting for data.

All modern processors use at least one level of cache: a copy of the RAM held in the processor that can be very quickly manipulated. Cache is typically fetched in pages; a whole section of main memory is streamed to the processor. It can then be manipulated at will. When the processor has done its work, the cached memory is sent back to the main memory. The processor typically cannot work on the main memory: All the memory it needs must be on cache. An operating system may add additional complexity to this, as a memory request may have to pass through an operating system routine that translates the request into a request for real or virtual memory. This can introduce further constraints, as two bits of physical memory with a similar mapped address might not be available at the same time (called an *aliasing failure*).

Multiple levels of cache work the same way as a single cache. A large amount of memory is fetched to the lowest level cache, a subset of that is fetched to each higher-level cache, and the processor only ever works on the highest level.

If an algorithm uses data spread around memory, then it is unlikely that the right memory will be in the cache from moment to moment. These cache misses are costly in time. The processor has to fetch a whole new chunk of memory into the cache for one or two instructions, then it has to stream it all back out and request another block. A good profiling system will show when cache misses are happening. In my experience, even in languages that don't give you control over memory layout, dramatic speedups can be achieved by making sure that all the data needed for one algorithm are kept in the same place, in the same few objects.

In a game with 1,000 characters, it may be better to keep all their positions together in an array, so algorithms that make calculations based on location don't need to constantly jump around memory. As with all optimizations, profiling is everything, but a general level of efficiency can be gained by programming with data coherence in mind.

PLATFORMS

With the centralization of the industry around a few game engines, platform differences have less of an impact on AI design than they used to. Graphics programmers may still have to worry about console versus mobile, for example. But AI programming tends to be more general. In this section, I will consider each of the major platforms for games, highlighting any issues specific to AI code.

PC

PCs can be the most powerful games machines, with hard-core gamers buying high-end expensive hardware. But they can be frustrating for developers because of their lack of consistency. Where a console has fixed hardware (or at least relatively few variations), there is a bewildering array of different configurations for PCs. There is a vast difference between a machine with a pair of top of the range video cards, SSD drives and fast memory, and a budget PC with integrated graphics.

Things are easier than they were: Low-level developers rely on application programming interfaces (APIs) such as Vulkan and DirectX to insulate them from most hardware specifics, but the game still needs to detect feature support and speed and adjust accordingly. Developers working in an engine such as Unity and Unreal have it even easier, but may still need to use the built-in feature detection to ensure their game runs well on all systems.

Working with PCs involves building software that can scale from a casual gamer's limited system to the hard-core fan's up-to-date hardware. For graphics, this scaling can be reasonably modular; for example, for low-specification machines, we switch off advanced rendering features. A simpler shadow algorithm might be used, or physically based shaders might be replaced by simple texture mapping. A change in graphics sophistication usually doesn't change gameplay.

AI is different. If the AI gets less time to work, how should it respond? It can try to perform less work. This is effectively the same as having more stupid AI and can affect the difficulty level of the game. It is probably not acceptable to have your game be easier on lower-specification machines. Similarly, if we try to perform the same amount of work, it might take longer. This can mean a lower frame rate, or it can mean more frames between characters making decisions. Slow-to-react characters are also often easier to play against and can cause the same problems with QA.

The solution used by most developers is to target AI at the lowest common denominator: the minimum-specification machine listed in the technical design document. The AI time doesn't scale at all with the capabilities of the machine. Faster machines simply use proportionally less of their processing budget on AI.

There are many games, however, where scalable AI is feasible. Many games use AI to control ambient characters: pedestrians walking along the sidewalk, members of the crowd cheering a race, or flocks of birds swarming in the sky. This kind of AI is freely scalable: More characters can be used when the processor time is available.

CONSOLE

Consoles can be simpler to work with than a PC. You know exactly the machine you are targeting, and you can usually see code in operation on your target machine. There is no future proofing for new hardware or ever-changing versions of APIs to worry about.

Developers working with next-generation technology often don't have the exact specs of the final machine or a reliable hardware platform (initial development kits are often little more than a dedicated emulator), but most console development has a fairly fixed target.

The technical requirements checklist (TRC) process, by which a console manufacturer places minimum standards on the operation of a game, serves to fix things like frame rates (although different territories may vary—PAL and NTSC, for example). This means that AI budgets can be locked down in terms of a fixed number of milliseconds. In turn, this makes it much easier to work out what algorithms can be used and to have a fixed target for optimization (provided that the budget isn't slashed at the last milestone to make way for the latest graphics technique used in a competitor's game).

The same game engines used for PC development target consoles, making cross-platform development much easier than it has been in the past. Fortunately, few AI developers creating games are now working with the low-level details of a particular console. Almost all the low-level code is handled by engines or middleware.

MOBILE

Apple launched the iPhone in 2007, ushering in a revolution in gaming as big as anything since the home consoles of the 1980s. In 2006, mobile gaming consisted of dedicated handheld consoles like the PlayStation Portable (PSP) and Nintendo's Game Boy Advance. Now almost 100% of the market is for phones and tablets.

There are two platforms in the space: Apple, with its iOS devices (iPhone, iPad, iPod Touch), and Android. Until recently, these were very different, and required games to be coded for each individually. Although both can use low-level languages such as C and C++, for higher-level languages Apple encourages the use of Swift (it formerly used Objective-C), and Android Java (or languages that compile into Java bytecode, such as Kotlin).

Both the major game engines by market share (Unreal and Unity), as well as many smaller competitors (e.g., Godot), support mobile platforms with the same game code, making platform-specific implementation unnecessary. There has been a big shift toward mobile developers working in a cross-platform way, using these tools. Factoring in the Steam platform as a viable marketplace for mobile games running on PC, I think there is no doubt this trend will soon become almost ubiquitous.

Smartphones capable of running games are powerful machines, comparable to last-generation consoles and PCs 5–10 years old. There is no longer any practical difference between the kinds of AI that can be run on a PC or console and those that can be run on mobile. Phones may require simpler graphics or smaller crowd sizes, but in terms of algorithms, the same things now apply.

VIRTUAL AND AUGMENTED REALITY

In early 2019, virtual and augmented reality are both extremely hyped, and a tiny proportion of the games market. The technology and the market is in rapid flux, and beyond generalities, very little that could be said now would be true in 2 years.

Virtual reality (VR) attempts to immerse the player in the game world by providing a stereoscopic 3D point of view. Depending on the hardware, a player's motion may also be detected and incorporated as movement in the game. VR requires separate views of the scene to be rendered for each eye, and to avoid motion sickness, higher frame rates are typically targeted (90fps, for example).

Up to this point, most virtual reality devices have been displays tethered to an existing games machine, such as a PC (Oculus Rift and Vive), a console (PlayStation VR), or a phone (Gear VR). At the time of writing, companies are beginning to release stand-alone VR products, based on mobile processors, with approximately similar performance to high-end phones.

Augmented reality (AR) uses semitransparent displays to add computer-generated elements to the real world. Although Microsoft released a development kit in early 2016, a consumer version has not yet followed. Magic Leap released their product in 2018, but saw limited demand. Augmented reality may also refer to games that use a mobile phone camera, and add computer-generated elements to the captured images. In that sense, *Pokémon Go*, for example, is considered an augmented reality game, but does not require specialist hardware.

While the visual presentation of VR games may be unconventional, the game logic rarely is. Most commercial game engines support VR, AR on mobile via camera, and are positioned to offer hardware AR support, when products are announced. VR and AR games are similar enough in design not to need unusual AI algorithms. It remains to be seen whether these platforms open new design possibilities. It also remains to be seen whether these platforms become a significant part of the industry.

THE AI ENGINE

When I started in the industry, a game was mostly built from scratch. Some bits of code were dragged from previous projects, and some bits were reworked and reused, but most were new. A handful of companies used the same basic code to write multiple games, as long as the games were a similar style and genre. LucasArts' SCUMM engine, for example, was a gradually evolving game engine used to power many point-and-click adventure games.

Since then, game engines have become ubiquitous, a consistent technical platform on which multiple games are built. Low-level routines (like talking to the operating system, loading textures, model file formats, and so on) are shared among all titles, a set of tools are available for a broad range of games (e.g., 2D graphics, 3D graphics, and networking), and finally, interfaces are provided to add game-specific code on top. Originally, these engines belonged to individual companies, but over time, only the very largest companies could afford to keep their engines up-to-date. It is now common for large developers to license commercial engines.

The way AI is developed has changed, also. Initially, the AI was written for each game and sometimes for each character. Now there is an increasing tendency to have general AI routines, either built into the game engine, available to license as commercial add-ons, or created and reused in-house by a developer. This allows individual characters to be designed by level editors, game designers, or technical artists. The engine structure is fixed, and the AI for each character combines the components in an appropriate way.

So, building a game engine involves building AI tools that can be easily reused, combined, and applied in interesting ways. To support this, we need an AI structure that makes sense over multiple genres.

STRUCTURE OF AN AI ENGINE

In my experience, there are a few basic facilities that need to be in place for a general AI system. They conform to the model of AI given in Figure 4.1.

First, we must have some kind of infrastructure in two categories: a general mechanism for managing AI behaviors (deciding which behavior gets to run when, and so on) and a world interfacing

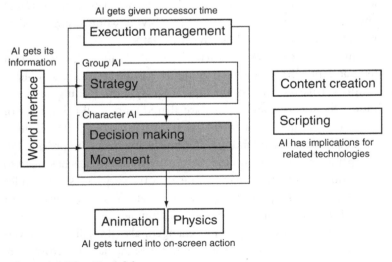

Figure 4.1 The AI model.

system for getting information into the AI. Every AI algorithm needs to honor these mechanisms.

Second, we must have a means to turn whatever the AI wants to do into action on-screen. This consists of standard interfaces to a movement and an animation controller, which can turn requests such as "pull lever 1" or "walk stealthily to position x, y" into action.

Third, a standard behavior structure must serve as a liaison between the two. It is almost guaranteed that you will need to write one or two AI algorithms for each new game. Having all AI conform to the same structure helps this immensely. New code can be in development while the game is running, and the new AI can simply replace placeholder behaviors when it is ready.

All this needs to be thought out in advance. The structure needs to be in place before you get well into your AI coding. Chapter 6 of this book describes support technologies, which are the first thing to implement in an AI engine. The individual techniques can then slot in.

Game engines do some of this for you, but not all. Each engine has its own mechanism to make sure your code is run, often in the form of base classes that you should derive from. But you may need to provide more fine-grained control: Not every character needs its AI run in every frame. They also provide standard mechanisms for scheduling animations, but less often character movement. And they may provide basic tools for working out which character knows what (such as a built-in line of sight or sight cone check), but will need custom implementations for anything more complex. Unless you intend to use very simple techniques, you will need to create some infrastructure, and possibly some tools in the editor to support it.

There are techniques that can work on their own, and all the algorithms are fairly independent. For a demo, or a simple game, it might be sufficient to just use the technique. But a good AI structure helps promote reuse and reduces debugging and development time.

TOOL CONCERNS

The complete AI engine will have a central pool of AI algorithms that can be applied to many characters. The definition for a particular character's AI will therefore consist of data (which may include scripts in some scripting language), rather than compiled code. The data specify how a character is put together: What techniques will be used and how those techniques are parameterized and combined.

These data need to come from somewhere. Data can be manually created, but this is no better than writing the AI by hand each time. Flexible tools ensure that the artists and designers can create the content in an easy way, while allowing the content to be inserted into the game without manual help. These are usually created as custom modes in the game engine editor: a tool for setting up character decision-making rules, or an overlay onto the level used to mark tactical locations or places to avoid.

The need to expose search tools has its own effect on the choice of AI techniques. It is easy to set up behaviors that always act the same way. Steering behaviors are a good example: They tend to be very simple, they are easily parameterized (with the physical capabilities of a character), and they do not change from character to character.

It is more difficult to use behaviors that have lots of conditions, where the character needs to evaluate special cases. Those based on a tree (decision trees and behavior trees) are easier to represent visually. A rule-based system, on the other hand, needs to have complicated matching rules defined. When these are supported in a tool, they typically look like program code, because a programming language is the most natural way to express them.

PUTTING IT ALL TOGETHER

The final structure of the AI engine might look something like Figure 4.2. Data are created in a tool (the modeling or level editor), which is then packaged for use in the game. When a level is loaded, the game AI behaviors are created from level data and registered with

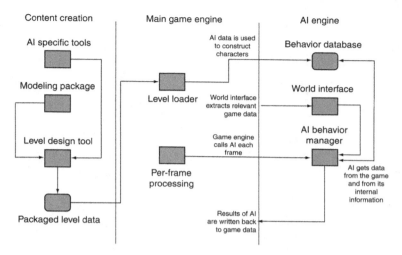

Figure 4.2 AI schematic.

the AI engine. During gameplay, the main game code calls the AI engine which updates the behaviors, getting information from the world interface and finally applying their output to the game data.

The particular techniques used depend heavily on the genre of the game being developed. As you develop your game AI, you'll need to take a mix and match approach to get the behaviors you are looking for.

5

TECHNIQUES

MOVEMENT

One of the most fundamental requirements of game AI is to sensibly move characters around. Even the earliest AI-controlled characters (the ghosts in Pac-Man, for example, or the opposing bat in some Pong variants) had movement algorithms that weren't far removed from modern games.

Movement forms the lowest level of AI techniques in our model, as shown in Figure 5.1.

Many games, including some with quite decent-looking AI, rely solely on movement algorithms and don't have any more advanced decision-making. At the other extreme, some games don't need moving characters at all. Resource management games and turn-based games often don't need movement algorithms; once a decision is made where to move, the character can simply be placed there.

There is also some degree of overlap between AI and animation; animation is also about movement. This chapter looks at large-scale movement: the movement of characters around the game level, rather than the movement of their limbs or faces. The dividing line isn't always clear, however. In many games, animation can take control over a character, including some large-scale movement. This may be as simple as the character moving a few steps to pull a lever. Or

DOI: 10.1201/9781003124047-6

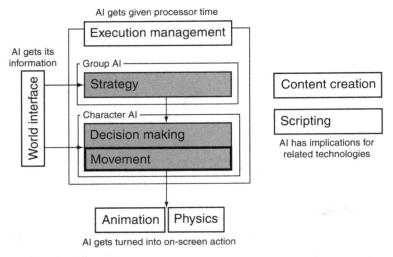

Figure 5.1 The AI model.

as complex as mini cut-scenes, completely animated, that seamlessly transition into and out of gameplay.

THE BASICS OF MOVEMENT ALGORITHMS

Unless you're writing an economic simulator, chances are the characters in your game need to move around. Each character has a current position and possibly additional physical properties that control its movement. A movement algorithm is designed to use these properties to work out where the character should be next.

All movement algorithms have this same basic form. They take geometric data about their own state and the state of the world, and they come up with a geometric output representing the movement they would like to make. Figure 5.2 shows this schematically. In the figure, the velocity of a character is shown as optional because it is only needed for certain classes of movement algorithms.

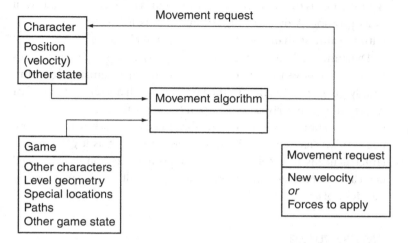

Figure 5.2 The movement algorithm structure.

Some movement algorithms require very little input: just the position of the character and the position of an enemy to chase, for example. Others require a lot of interaction with the game state and the level geometry. A movement algorithm that avoids bumping into walls, for example, needs to have access to the geometry of the wall to check for potential collisions.

The output can vary too. In most games, it is normal to have movement algorithms output a desired velocity. A character might see its enemy to the west, for example, and respond that its movement should be westward at full speed. Often, characters in older games only had two speeds: stationary and running (with maybe a walk speed in there, too, for patrolling). So the output was simply a direction to move in. This is kinematic movement; it does not account for how characters accelerate and slow down.

It is common now for more physical properties to be taken into account. Producing movement algorithms I will call "steering behaviors." They are not kinematic, but dynamic. Dynamic movement takes account of the current motion of the character. A dynamic algorithm typically needs to know the current velocities of the character as well as its position. A dynamic algorithm outputs forces or accelerations with the aim of changing the velocity of the character.

Dynamics adds an extra layer of complexity. Let's say your character needs to move from one place to another. A kinematic algorithm simply gives the direction to the target; your character moves in that direction until it arrives, whereupon the algorithm returns no direction. A dynamic movement algorithm needs to work harder. It first needs to accelerate in the right direction, and then as it gets near its target it needs to accelerate in the opposite direction, so its speed decreases at precisely the correct rate to slow it to a stop at exactly the right place.

PATHFINDING

Game characters usually need to move around their level. Sometimes this movement is set in stone by the developers, such as a patrol route that a guard can follow blindly or a small fenced region in which a dog can randomly wander around. Fixed routes are simple to implement, but can easily be fooled if an object is pushed in the way. Free wandering characters can appear aimless and can easily get stuck.

More complex characters don't know in advance where they'll need to move. A unit in a real-time strategy game may be ordered to any point on the map by the player at any time, a patrolling guard in a stealth game may need to move to its nearest alarm point to call for reinforcements, and a platform game may require opponents to chase the player across a chasm using available platforms.

For each of these characters, the AI must be able to calculate a suitable route through the game level to get from where it is now to its goal. We'd like the route to be sensible and as short or rapid as possible (it doesn't look smart if your character walks from the kitchen to the lounge via the attic).

This is pathfinding, sometimes called path planning, and it is everywhere in game AI.

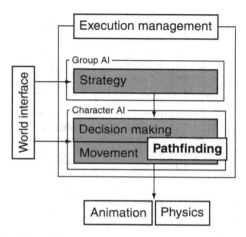

Figure 5.3 The AI model.

In our model of game AI (Figure 5.3), pathfinding sits on the border between decision-making and movement. Often, it is used simply to work out where to move to reach a goal; the goal is decided by another bit of AI, and the pathfinder simply works out how to get there. To accomplish this, it can be embedded in a movement control system so that it is only called when it is needed to plan a route. But pathfinding can also be placed in the driving seat, making decisions about where to move as well as how to get there.

The vast majority of games use pathfinding solutions based on an algorithm called A*. Although it's efficient and easy to implement, A* can't work directly with the game level data. It requires that the game level be represented in a particular data structure: a directed nonnegative weighted graph.

DECISION-MAKING

Ask a gamer about game AI, and they think about decision-making: the ability of a character to decide what to do. Carrying out that decision (movement, animation, and the like) is taken for granted.

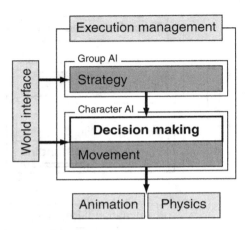

Figure 5.4 The AI model.

In reality, decision-making is typically a small part of the effort needed to build great game AI. Most games use simple decision-making systems: state machines and behavior trees. Rule-based systems are rarer, but important.

In recent years, a lot of interest has been shown in more sophisticated decision-making tools, such as fuzzy logic and neural networks. Despite notable uses in some high-profile games (often accompanied by much marketing fanfare), developers haven't been in a rush to embrace these technologies. It can be hard to get them working right. Decision-making is the middle component of our AI model (Figure 5.4).

OVERVIEW OF DECISION-MAKING

Although there are many different decision-making techniques, we can look at them all as acting in the same way.

The character processes a set of information that it uses to generate an action that it wants to carry out. The input to the decision-making system is the knowledge that a character possesses, and the output is an action request. The knowledge can be further broken down into external and internal knowledge. External knowledge is the information that a character knows about the game environment around it: the position of other characters, the layout of the level, whether a switch has been thrown, the direction that a noise is coming from, and so on. Internal knowledge is information about the character's internal state or thought processes: its health, its ultimate goals, what it was doing a couple of seconds ago, and so on.

Typically, the same knowledge can drive any of the algorithms in this chapter. Some internal data are particular to the algorithms themselves (a state machine needs to hold what state the character is currently in, for example, where a goal-oriented behavior needs to know what its current goal is). The algorithms themselves control what kinds of internal knowledge can be used (whether it stores goals, states, plans, or probabilities), although they don't constrain what that knowledge represents, in game terms.

The behavior of an algorithm, correspondingly, can affect the game in two ways: They can request an action that will change the external state of the character (such as throwing a switch, firing a weapon, and moving into a room), and they can change the internal state of the algorithm (such as adopting a new goal, or adjusting a probability). See Figure 5.5 for a schematic representation of this.

Changes to the internal state are, by definition, less visible to the player, in the same way that changes in a person's mental state are not visible unless they act on them. But in most decision-making algorithms, the internal state is where most of the work is done. Changes might correspond to altering the character's opinion of the player, changing its emotional state, or adopting a new goal. Again, algorithms will typically carry out those internal changes in a way that is particular to the algorithm, while external actions can be generated in a form that is identical for each algorithm.

The format and quantity of the knowledge available to the AI depend on the requirements of the game. Knowledge representation is intrinsically linked with most decision-making algorithms. It is difficult to be completely general with knowledge representation.

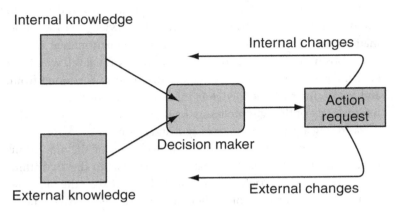

Figure 5.5 Decision-making schematic.

TACTICAL AND STRATEGIC AI

The decision-making techniques we looked at in the last chapter have two important limitations: They are intended for use by a single character, and they don't try to infer from the knowledge they have to a prediction of the whole situation.

Each of these limitations is broadly in the category of tactics and strategy. This chapter looks at techniques that provide a framework for tactical and strategic reasoning in characters. It includes methods to deduce the tactical situation from sketchy information, to use the tactical situation to make decisions, and to coordinate between multiple characters.

In the model of AI I've been using so far, this provides the third layer of our system, as shown in Figure 5.6.

It is worth remembering again that not all parts of the model are needed in every game. Tactical and strategic AI, in particular, is simply not needed in many game genres. Where players expect to see predictable behavior (in a two-dimensional [2D] shooter or a platform game, for example), it may simply frustrate them to face more complex behaviors.

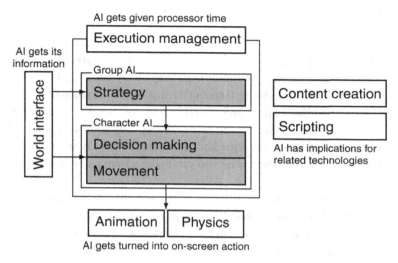

Figure 5.6 The AI model.

There has been a rapid increase in the tactical capabilities of AI-controlled characters over the last 10 years, partly because of the increase in AI budgets and processor speeds, and partly due to the adoption of simple techniques that can bring impressive results, as we'll see in this chapter. It is an exciting and important area to be working in, and there is no sign of that changing.

LEARNING

Machine learning (often abbreviated ML, though in this book I will simply call it "learning") is a hot topic in technology and business, and that excitement has filtered into games. In principle, learning AI has the potential to adapt to each player, learning their tricks and techniques and providing a consistent challenge. It has the potential to produce more believable characters: characters that can learn about their environment and use it to the best effect. It also has the potential to reduce the effort needed to create game-specific AI:

Characters should be able to learn about their surroundings and the tactical options that they provide.

In practice, it hasn't yet fulfilled its promise, and not for want of trying. Applying learning to your game requires careful planning and an understanding of the pitfalls. There have been some impressive successes in building learning AI that learns to play games, but less in providing compelling characters or enemies. The potential is sometimes more attractive than the reality, but if you understand the quirks of each technique and are realistic about how you apply them, there is no reason why you can't take advantage of learning in your game.

There is a whole range of different learning techniques, from very simple number tweaking through to complex neural networks. While most of the attention in the last few years has been focused on "deep learning" (a form of neural networks), there are many other practical approaches. Each has its own idiosyncrasies that need to be understood before they can be used in real games.

LEARNING BASICS

We can classify learning techniques into several groups depending on when the learning occurs, what is being learned, and what effects the learning has on a character's behavior.

ONLINE OR OFFLINE LEARNING

Learning can be performed during the game, while the player is playing. This is online learning, and it allows the characters to adapt dynamically to the player's style and provides more consistent challenges. As a player plays more, their characteristic traits can be better anticipated by the computer, and the behavior of characters can be tuned to playing styles. This might be used to make enemies pose an ongoing challenge, or it could be used to offer the player more story lines of the kind they enjoy playing.

Unfortunately, online learning also produces problems with predictability and testing. If the game is constantly changing, it can be difficult to replicate bugs and problems. If an enemy character decides that the best way to tackle the player is to run into a wall, then it can be a nightmare to replicate the behavior (at worst you'd have to play through the whole same sequence of games, doing exactly the same thing each time as the player).

The majority of learning in game AI is done offline, either between levels of the game or more often at the development studio before the game leaves the building. This is performed by processing data about real games and trying to calculate strategies or parameters from them.

This allows more unpredictable learning algorithms to be tried out and their results to be tested exhaustively. The learning algorithms in games are usually applied offline; it is rare to find games that use any kind of online learning. Learning algorithms are increasingly being used offline to learn tactical features of multi-player maps, to produce accurate pathfinding and movement data, and to bootstrap interaction with physics engines. These are very constrained applications. Studios are experimenting with using deep learning in a broader way, having characters learn higher behavior from scratch. It remains to be seen whether this is successful enough to make major inroads into the way AI is created.

Applying learning in the pause when loading the next level of the game is a kind of offline learning: Characters aren't learning as they are acting. But it has many of the same downsides as online learning. We need to keep it short (load times for levels are usually part of a publisher or console manufacturer's acceptance criteria for a game and certainly affects player satisfaction). We need to take care that bugs and problems can be replicated without replaying tens of games. We need to make sure that the data from the game are easily available in a suitable format (we can't use long post-processing steps to dig data out of a huge log file, for example).

Most of the techniques in this chapter can be applied either online or offline. They aren't limited to one or the other. If they are to be applied online, then the data they will learn from are presented as they are generated by the game. If it is used offline, then the data are stored and pulled in as a whole later.

INTRA-BEHAVIOR LEARNING

The simplest kinds of learning are those that change a small area of a character's behavior. They don't change the whole quality of the behavior, but simply tweak it a little. These intra-behavior learning techniques are easy to control and can be easy to test.

Examples include learning to target correctly when projectiles are modeled by accurate physics, learning the best patrol routes around a level, learning where cover points are in a room, and learning how to chase an evading character successfully. Most of the learning examples in this chapter will illustrate intra-behavior learning.

An intra-behavior learning algorithm doesn't help a character work out that it needs to do something very different (if a character is trying to reach a high ledge by learning to run and jump, it won't tell the character to simply use the stairs instead, for example).

INTER-BEHAVIOR LEARNING

The frontier for learning AI in games is learning of behavior. What I mean by behavior is a qualitatively different mode of action—for example, a character that learns the best way to kill an enemy is to lay an ambush or a character that learns to tie a rope across a backstreet to stop an escaping motorbiker. Characters that can learn from scratch how to act in the game provide a challenging opposition for even the best human players.

Unfortunately, this kind of AI is on the limit of what might be possible.

Over time, an increasing amount of character behavior may be learned, either online or offline. Some of this may be to learn how to choose between a range of different behaviors (although the atomic behaviors will still need to be implemented by the developer). It is doubtful that it will be economical to learn everything. The basic movement systems, decision-making tools, suites of available behaviors, and high-level decision-making will almost certainly be easier and faster to implement directly. They can then be augmented with intra-behavior learning to tweak parameters.

The frontier for learning AI is decision-making. Developers are increasingly experimenting with replacing AI techniques with learning systems, in particular deep learning.

A WARNING

In reality, learning is not as widely used as you might think. Some of this is due to the relative complexity of learning techniques (in comparison with pathfinding and movement algorithms, at least). But games developers master far more complex techniques all the time, for graphics, network, and physics simulation. The biggest problems with learning are not difficulty, but reproducibility and quality control.

Imagine a game in which the enemy characters learn their environment and the player's actions over the course of several hours of gameplay. While playing one level, the QA team notices that a group of enemies is stuck in one cavern, not moving around the whole map. It is possible that this condition occurs only as a result of the particular set of things they have learned. In this case, finding the bug and later testing if it has been fixed involves replaying the same learning experiences. This is often impossible.

It is this kind of unpredictability that is the most often cited reason for severely curbing the learning ability of game characters. As companies developing industrial learning AI have often found, it is impossible to avoid the AI learning the "wrong" thing.

When you read academic papers about learning and games, they often use dramatic scenarios to illustrate the potential of a learning character on gameplay. You need to ask yourself, if the character can learn such dramatic changes of behavior, then can it also learn dramatically poor behavior: behavior that might fulfill its own goals but will produce terrible gameplay? You can't have your cake and eat it. The more flexible your learning is, the less control you have on gameplay.

The normal solution to this problem is to constrain the kinds of things that can be learned in a game. It is sensible to limit a particular learning system to working out places to take cover, for example. This learning system can then be tested by making sure that the cover points it is identifying look right. The learning will have difficulty getting carried away; it has a single task that can be easily visualized and checked.

Under this modular approach, there is nothing to stop several different learning systems from being applied (one for cover points, another to learn accurate targeting, and so on). Care must be taken to ensure that they can't interact in nasty ways. The targeting AI may learn to shoot in such a way that it often accidentally hits the cover that the cover-learning AI is selecting, for example.

OVER-LEARNING

A common problem identified in much of the AI learning literature is over-fitting, or over-learning. This means that if a learning AI is exposed to a number of experiences and learns from them, it may learn the response to only those situations. We normally want the learning AI to be able to generalize from the limited number of experiences it has to be able to cope with a wide range of new situations.

Different algorithms have different susceptibilities to over-fitting. Neural networks particularly can over-fit during learning if they are wrongly parameterized or if the network is too large for the learning task at hand. We'll return to these issues as we consider each learning algorithm in turn.

THE BALANCE OF EFFORT

The key thing to remember in all learning algorithms is the balance of effort. Learning algorithms are attractive because you can do less implementation work. You don't need to anticipate every eventuality or make the character AI particularly good. Instead, you create a general-purpose learning tool and allow that to find the really tricky solutions to the problem. The balance of effort should be that it is less work to get the same result by creating a learning algorithm to do some of the work.

Unfortunately, it is often not possible. Learning algorithms can require a lot of hand-holding: presenting data in the correct way, parameterizing the learning system, making sure their results are valid, and testing them to avoid them learning the wrong thing.

I advise developers to consider carefully the balance of effort involved in learning. If a technique is very tricky for a human being to solve and implement, then it is likely to be tricky for the computer, too. If a human being can't reliably learn to keep a car cornering on the limit of its tire's grip, then a computer is unlikely to suddenly find it easy when equipped with a vanilla learning algorithm. To get the result, you likely have to do a lot of additional work. Great results in academic papers can be achieved by the researchers carefully selecting the problem they need to solve, and spending a lot of time fine-tuning the solution. Both are luxuries a studio AI developer cannot afford.

PROCEDURAL CONTENT GENERATION

Procedural content generation is a hot topic in game development. But it is not new. Its use goes back to the 8-bit era of the 1980s. Both *Elite* and *Exile* generated a sizable portion of their content (in the first case a whole galaxy of stars; in the second an underground cave system). Both games were the same each time you played, but the game content was far too big to fit in the 32 kB of RAM available. They used procedural generation as a form of compression. Elite in particular proved highly influential, directly leading to games such as *Spore*, *Elite: Dangerous*, and *No Man's Sky*.

In the early 1980s, *Rogue* was first released as freeware for mainframe machines. It featured a procedurally generated dungeon that was different on each play, and permadeath so a level couldn't be repeated over and over until it was beaten. Rogue led to many other noncommercial and hobbyist games, often using similar pure text interfaces. The genre became known as Rogue-likes. Procedural content generation and permadeath crossed into independent commercial games, becoming a phenomenon with titles such as *The Binding of Isaac* and *Spelunky*, a burgeoning genre that came to be known as Rogue-lites. Procedural dungeon generation even featured in AAA titles such as *Diablo* and the chalice dungeons of *Bloodborne*.

Spore also draws on another thread of procedural content generation: the demo scene. Participants compete to produce the most spectacular audio and visual show, often based on highly constrained program sizes. This is often a combination of both shaving the size of an executable with hand-optimized assembly code, and generating the audio and much of the visuals with procedural content generation. Will Wright, the creator of *Spore*, recruited prominent demo scene coders to work on that game.

Strategy games such as *Civilization*, and its sequels, use procedural level generation to create varied maps for multi-player games. Landscape generation is ubiquitous enough that most game artists use some kind of content generation—possibly with human modification—to create terrain, even in games with fixed levels. This is procedural content generation used in the studio, rather than running on the game machine. *Minecraft* brought landscape and world generation to a huge audience. Building on a simple block-based structure, Mojang over time has added generation routines to create mines, villages, temples, and other structures, each intended to evoke the feel of something man-made.

And finally, in a survey of games, it would be remiss not to give due credit to *Dwarf Fortress*, in some ways a game that owes a lot to *Rogue*, particularly in its aesthetics, but where procedural content generation has been pushed into all systems. The world is generated, as are dungeons, characters, back stories, civilizations, even legends, and artifacts. A book in this series contains procedural content generation advice, co-edited by the co-author of *Dwarf Fortress*.

This survey of procedural content generation illustrates its two main uses: in game, to generate variety; and during development, to make game assets higher fidelity or cheaper to create. In both cases, it replaces the work that would otherwise be done by a designer or an artist. It is, therefore, an AI task. And unsurprisingly, it uses techniques similar to those already covered in this book. In some cases, the connection can be more tenuous. Similarly, game textures are often procedurally generated, but methods for achieving this are based on image filtering and graphical programming techniques. At the other extreme, games such as *Left 4 Dead* and *Earthfall* generate gameplay moments using a "director" AI: decision-making that analyses the state of the game and schedules new enemies and encounters to keep it interesting and challenging to the player.

BOARD GAMES

The earliest application of AI to computer games was as opponents in simulated versions of common board games. In the West, Chess is the archetypal board game, and the last 40 years have seen a dramatic increase in the capabilities of Chess-playing computers.

In the same time frame, other games such as Tic-Tac-Toe, Connect Four, Reversi (Othello), and Go have been studied, in each case culminating in AI that can beat the best human opponents.

The AI techniques needed to make a computer play board games are very different. For the real-time games that dominate the charts, this kind of AI only has limited applicability. It is occasionally used as a strategic layer, making long-term decisions in war games, but even then only when the game has been designed to be somewhat board game like.

The best AI opponents for Go, Chess, Draughts, Backgammon, and Reversi—those capable of beating the best human players—have all used dedicated hardware, algorithms, or optimizations devised specifically for the nuances of their strategy. This may be changing. With the advent of deep learning board game AI, particularly those created by the company DeepMind, there is some indication that elite-level approaches can be applied to multiple games. As of writing, it remains to be seen whether the success can be replicated by others, or whether even better results can be achieved by further specialization.

For all these games, however, the basic underlying algorithms are shared in common, and can find application in any board game. The minimax family of algorithms is the most popular board game AI techniques. A different family of algorithms has proven to be superior in many applications: the memory-enhanced test driver (MTD) algorithms. Both minimax and MTD are tree-search algorithms: They require a special tree representation of the game.

These algorithms are perfect for implementing the AI in board games, but both rely on some knowledge of the game. The algorithms are designed to search for the best move to make, but the computer can't intuit what "best" means; it needs to be told. At its simplest, this can be just "the best move wins the game," which is all we need for a game like Tic-Tac-Toe, where minimax or MTD can search every possible sequence of moves. But for most games, there isn't enough computer power to search all the way to the end of the game, so some knowledge about intermediate states is needed: The best moves lead to the best positions, so how do we determine how good a position is? We use a "static evaluation function."

This is the same trade-off I introduced as the "golden rule of AI," when discussing symbolic AI in Chapter 1: The more search we can do, the less knowledge we need, and vice versa. In the case of reasonably complicated board games, the amount of search we can do is limited by the computer power available; better search algorithms only buy us a little. So the quality of the AI will depend more on the quality of the static evaluation function.

6

SUPPORTING TECHNOLOGIES

EXECUTION MANAGEMENT

There are only limited processor resources available to a game. Traditionally, most of these have been used to create great graphics: the primary driving force in mass-market games. Much of the hard graphical processing is now performed on the GPU, but not all of it. Faster CPUs have also allowed the processor budget given to AI developers to grow steadily, meaning that techniques too costly at one time can now be implemented on even modest mobile hardware. It is not unheard of for AI to have more than 50% of the processor time, although 5%–25% is a more common range.

Even with more execution time available, processor time can easily get eaten up by pathfinding, complex decision-making, and tactical analysis. AI is also inherently inconsistent. Sometimes you need lots of time to make a decision (planning a route, for example), and sometimes a tiny budget is enough (moving along the route). All your characters may need to pathfind at the same time, and then you may have hundreds of frames where nothing much is happening to the AI.

A good AI system needs facilities that can make the best use of the limited processing time available. There are three main elements to this: dividing up the execution time among the AI that needs it, having algorithms that can work a bit at a time over several frames, and, when resources are scarce, giving preferential treatment to important characters.

DOI: 10.1201/9781003124047-7

The solution is motivated by AI, and without complex AI it is rarely needed. But developers with a good AI scheduling system tend to use it for many other purposes, too. I have seen a range of applications for the good scheduling infrastructure: incremental loading of new areas of the level, texture management, game logic, audio scheduling, and physics updates all controlled by scheduling systems originally designed with AI in mind.

WORLD INTERFACING

One of the most difficult things to get right as an AI developer is the interaction between the AI and the game world.

Each character needs to get the information they could feasibly know or perceive from the game world at the right time in order for them to act on it. In addition, some algorithms need to have information from the world represented in the correct way for them to process correctly.

To build a general-purpose AI system, we need to have some infrastructure that makes it easy to get the right information to the right bits of AI code in the right format at the right time. With a special-purpose, single-game AI, there may be no dividing line between the world interface and the AI code: If the AI needs some information, it can go and find it there and then. In an engine designed to support AI in multiple games, however, it is essential for stability and reusability to have a single central world interface system. Even within one game, it can dramatically assist debugging to have all the information flowing through a central hub, allowing it to be visualized, logged, and inspected.

TOOLS AND CONTENT CREATION

Programming makes up a relatively small amount of the effort in a mass-market game. Most of the development time goes into content creation, making models, textures, environments, sounds, music, and animation—everything from the concept art to the fine-tuning of the level.

Over the last 15 years, developers have reduced the programming effort further by reusing technology on multiple titles, creating or licensing a game engine on which several games can run. Adding a comprehensive suite of AI to the engine is a natural extension.

Most developers aren't content to stop there, however. Because the effort involved in content creation is so great, the content creation process also needs to be standardized, and the runtime tools need to be seamlessly integrated with development tools. For more than a decade, these complete toolchains have been essential for development of large games. With the explosion in popularity of the Unity engine, they have become crucial to the existence of small studios, independent developers, and hobbyists.

In fact, it is difficult to overstate the importance of the toolchain in modern game development. At the time of the first edition of this book, the toolchain was seen as a major deciding factor in a publisher's decisions to back a project. Now it is almost ubiquitous. It is a rare and brave developer indeed that creates a new game from scratch without a proven toolchain in place.

Partly, this is due to their availability. RenderWare Studio was a major selling point for Criterion's graphics middleware in the early 2000s. But licensing it was costly and required a detailed agreement with a vendor. Now it is trivial to download Unity or Unreal Engine from the web, experiment under a simple end user license, and have access to a widely supported and powerful toolchain. These tools are not free, but their ease of use has transformed the industry. In addition to these two market leaders, other systems such as the open-source Godot and Amazon's Lumberyard (a fork of the Crytek's CryEngine) also emphasize the same style of game development, with the toolchain and a custom editor application at the core.

TOOLCHAINS LIMIT AI

The importance of toolchains places limits on the AI. Advanced techniques such as neural networks, genetic algorithms, and goal-oriented action planning (GOAP) haven't been widely used in commercial titles. To some degree, this is because they are naturally difficult to map into a level editing tool. They require specific programming for a character, which limits the speed at which new levels can be created and the code reuse between projects.

The majority of AI-specific design tools are concerned with the bread-and-butter techniques: finite state machines or behavior trees, movement, and pathfinding. These approaches rely on simple processes and significant knowledge. Toolchains are naturally better at allowing designers to modify data rather than code, so the use of these classic techniques is being reinforced.

WHERE AI KNOWLEDGE COMES FROM

Good AI requires a lot of knowledge. Having good and appropriate knowledge about the game environment saves a huge amount of processing time. And at runtime, when the game has many things to keep track of, processing time is a crucial resource.

The knowledge required by AI algorithms depends on the environment of the game. A character moving around, for example, needs some knowledge of where and how it is possible to move. This can be provided by the programmers, giving the AI the data it needs directly.

When the game level changes, however, the programmer needs to provide new sets of data. This does not promote reuse between multiple games and makes it difficult for simple changes to be made to levels. A toolchain approach to developing a game puts the onus on the content creation team to provide the necessary AI knowledge. This process can be aided by offline processing which automatically produces a database of knowledge from the raw level information.

For years, it has been common for the content creation team to provide the AI knowledge for movement and pathfinding, either explicitly by marking up the level itself or by having such data generated automatically from the content they create. More recently, decision-making and higher-level AI functions have also been incorporated into the toolchain, usually via custom tools integrated into the editor application.

PROGRAMMING GAME AI

Editors and other tools are important for content creation: building the data that give the game its gameplay, from the obvious visual design of the geometry of levels to the configuration of AI algorithms that make up character behavior. Different AI approaches will require different tools: extensions to level editing or 3D modeling, or custom tools for visualizing and configuring decision-making. The exact requirement depends on the approach being used.

In contrast, there is one tool that is always necessary, so much so that it can be easily ignored in a discussion of supporting technologies. All AI is programmed. And the programming language has a big impact on the design of the AI.

Pathfinding or decision trees, for example, are general approaches that can be used in a whole range of games. These techniques need to be implemented. A decade ago, it would not be unreasonable to assume that they would be implemented in C++ as part of the core game code. That has changed radically now. Although game engines are still usually implemented in C and C++, most of the AI is typically implemented in another language. The most common commercial game engines, Unity and Unreal Engine 4 (UE4), provide a pathfinding system written in C++, but if you need any other AI technique (a behavior tree, for example, or steering behaviors), it needs to be written, or licensed from a third party. In UE4, this may still involve coding in C++, but in Unity, it probably means implementing in C#. In both cases, the new code acts as a kind of plug-in, on equal footing with gameplay code rather than core facilities such as networking and 3D rendering.

At the same time, mobile and online development has burgeoned, where implementation languages are constrained by the target platform: Swift (and before that Objective-C) on iOS, Java (or other JVM languages such as Kotlin) on Android, and JavaScript on the web. Together, these trends have meant that AI techniques are being implemented in a much broader range of languages.

But general-purpose AI techniques are only one place in which AI code requires programming support. It is common to use small scripts written in an embedded programming language to control character behavior. Often this is easier than using a general-purpose technique, and developing tools to configure it correctly. Provided that the person creating the character behavior is reasonably confident with simple programming tasks, it might be much easier to produce state-based behavior with a series of if-statements rather than dragging blocks and transitions in a general purpose state machine editor.

Commercial game engines always provide some form of scripting support. If you are developing your tool set from scratch, you may need to add your own. Although increasingly rare, many developers have felt existing options are unsuitable, and developed their own scripting languages.

INDEX